welcome to...
THE
NEW EUROPE
DOSSIER

A LETTER FROM THE AUTHOR

Hello,

Europe is changing, and changing fast. More united than ever before, it's developing a powerful new identity as the twenty-first century approaches. This Dossier explores that new identity. How? By focusing on…

- European history since 1945
- life in Eastern Europe
- the past, present and future of the European Community
- the pros and cons of a twenty-first century 'Super-Europe'.

It also takes a wider look at European life in general, with articles about…

- language (from Dutch to Hungarian)
- cities (from Athens to Vienna)
- culture (from Leonardo da Vinci to the Eurovision Song Contest).

And even **that's** not all. On pages 30/31 there's an Action Section full of project ideas. For example, why not… (a) write a Euro-questionnaire, (b) give copies to people in your local community, (c) send the completed questionnaires to Brussels?

I hope you enjoy the New Europe Dossier and have fun with the Action Section. See you soon in another Macmillan Dossier. Until then,

Best wishes

Stephen Rabley

Stephen Rabley

DOSSIER SYMBOLS

Look out for these symbols

V look at the VOCAB BOX (there's one in every section)

BN look at the BACKGROUND NOTES (p32)

The European Flag

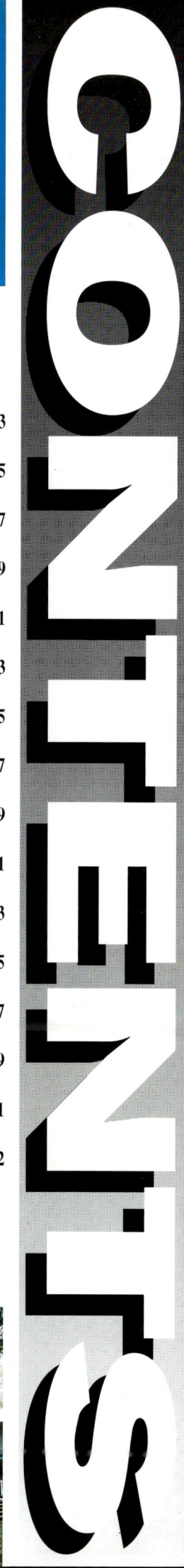

CONTENTS

The European Parliament at Strasbourg

THE EURO-FILE

An introduction to the nations of Europe.

The information contained in this section was checked by the publisher at the time of going to press, but is liable to change

Country	Capital	Other Cities	Official Language(s)	Currency	Area (Square Kilometres)	Population
Albania	Tirana	Shkodër, Vlorë, Durrës, Korçë	Albanian	New lek	28,750	3,200,000
Armenia	Yerevan	Leninakan, Kirovakan	Armenian	Rouble	30,000	3,283,000
Austria	Vienna	Graz, Linz, Salzburg, Innsbruck	German	Schilling	83,855	7,600,000
Azerbaijan	Baku	Kirovabad, Sumgait	Azerbaijani	Rouble	87,000	7,510,000
Belarus	Minsk	Gomel, Vitebsk, Mogilev	Belorussian	Rouble	208,000	10,200,000
Belgium	Brussels	Antwerp, Liège, Ghent, Bruges	French, German, Dutch	Belgian franc	30,520	9,913,000
Bosnia-Hercegovina	Sarajevo	Banja Luka, Tuzla, Mostar	Serbian, Croatian	Dinar	51, 129	4,479,000
Bulgaria	Sofia	Plovdiv, Burgas, Varna, Ruse	Bulgarian	Lev	110,910	8,970,000
Croatia	Zagreb	Rijeka, Split, Osijek, Karlovac	Croatian	Dinar	56,538	4,683,000
Cyprus	Nicosia	Limassol, Famagusta, Paphos, Akrotiri	Greek, Turkish	Cyprus pound	9,250	673,000
*Czech Republic	Prague	Brno, Plzen, Kladno, Ostrava	Czech	Koruna	78,922	10,350,480
Denmark	Copenhagen	Aarhus, Odense, Aalborg	Danish	Krone	43,069	5,140,000
Estonia	Tallinn	Tartu, Narva, Kohtla-Järve,	Estonian	Kroon	45,065	1,571,000
Finland	Helsinki	Tampere, Turku, Espoo, Vantaa	Finnish, Swedish	Finnish Mark	336,700	4,970,000
France	Paris	Lyons, Marseilles, Lille, Bordeaux	French	Franc	543,965	56,100,000
Georgia	Tbilisi	Sukhumi, Batumi, Kutaisi, Poti Rustavi	Georgian/ Russian	Rouble	70,000	6,379,000
Germany	Berlin	Frankfurt, Hamburg, Münich, Leipzig	German	German mark	357,849	79,670,000
Greece	Athens	Salonica, Piraeus, Heraklion	Greek	Drachma	131,985	10,000,000
Hungary	Budapest	Miskolc, Szeged, Pécs	Hungarian	Forint	93,030	10,611,000
Iceland	Reykjavik	Kopavogur, Akureyri, Keflavík	Icelandic	Krona	103,000	244,000
Ireland	Dublin	Cork, Limerick, Galway	English, Irish	Punt	68,895	3,537,195
Italy	Rome	Milan, Naples, Turin, Genoa	Italian	Lira	301,245	57,600,000
Latvia	Riga	Daugavpils, Liepaja, Jelgava, Ventspils	Latvian	Latvian Rouble	63,700	2,673,000
Liechtenstein	Vaduz	—	German	Swiss Franc	160	28,000
Lithuania	Vilnius	Kaunas, Klaipeda, Siauliai	Lithuanian	Rublis	67,806	3,641,000
Luxembourg	Luxembourg-ville	—	Letzeburgish, French, German	Luxembourg franc	2,586	400,000
Macedonia	Skopje	Kumanovo, Prilep, Bitola	Macedonian	Dinar	25,713	2,111,000
Malta	Valletta	Sliema	Maltese, English	Maltese lira	316	370,000
Moldova	Kishinev	Tiraspol, Beltsy, Bendery	Moldavian	Rouble	36,041	4,341,000
Monaco	Monaco-ville	—	French	French franc	1.90	29,876
Montenegro	Titograd	Cetinje, Nidšic, Pljevlja	Serbian	Dinar	13,812	639,000
Netherlands	Amsterdam[BN1]	The Hague, Rotterdam, Utrecht	Dutch	Guilder	41,785	14,890,000
Norway	Oslo	Bergen, Trondheim, Stavanger	Norwegian	Krone	323,895	4,190,758
Poland	Warsaw	Craców, Poznán, Gdańsk, Lódź	Polish	Zloty	312,685	38,200,000
Portugal	Lisbon	Oporto, Coímbra, Setúbal	Portuguese	Escudo	92,082	10,400,000
Romania	Bucharest	Timişoara, Braşon, Oradea, Iaşi	Romanian	Leu	237,500	23,174,000
Russia	Moscow	St. Petersburg, Gorky,	Russian	Rouble	17,075,400	147,386,000
Serbia	Belgrade	Novi Sad, Niš, Priština	Serbian	Dinar	55,968	9,830,000
*Slovakia	Bratislava	Košice, Banska, Bystrica, Zilina	Slovak	Koruna	48,954	5,108,800
Slovenia	Ljubljana	Celji, Maribor, Kranj, Novo Mesto	Slovenian	Tolar	20,246	1,891,864
Spain	Madrid	Barcelona, Valencia, Seville	Spanish	Peseta	504,880	39,075,000
Sweden	Stockholm	Gothenburg, Malmö, Uppsala	Swedish	Krona	449,790	8,500,000
Switzerland	Bern	Zurich, Basle, Geneva, Lausanne	German, French, Italian, Romansch	Swiss franc	41,290	6,738,197
Turkey	Ankara	Istanbul, Izmir, Adana, Mersin	Turkish	Turkish lira	779,450	55,400,000
Ukraine	Kiev	Odessa, Kharkov, Donetsk	Ukrainian	Rouble	652,969	51,704,000
United Kingdom	London	Belfast, Glasgow, Cardiff, Liverpool	English	Pound sterling	244,046	57,300,000
Vatican City	—	—	Italian, Latin	Vatican lira	0.44	755

* On 1 January 1993, Czechoslovakia became two states, the Czech Republic and Slovakia.

History...(1)

1 Greece

The Greek philosopher, Plato (see p22), with some of his students

Europe's first major culture existed on the Greek island of Crete from around 2000 BCᵛ to 1450 BC. This 'Minoan' civilisation had its own cities, roads and palaces (the most famous was at Knossos). Later – between the ninth and third centuries BC – another, even more advanced, Greek culture developed on the mainland. Its centre was the city of Athens and it's here that many important 'European' ideas about democracy, law, philosophy and art were born.

2 Rome

After Greece, Italy became the dominant nation. Foundedᵛ in 753 BC as a republic, Rome became powerful around 300 BC, and 200 years later it ruled almost the entire Mediterranean world. It was… (a) connected by a network of roads, (b) controlled by a huge army, (c) ruled (after 27 BC) by emperors, (d) one of the richest, most successful empires the world had ever seen. Yet even Rome couldn't last for ever. During the third and fourth centuries AD,ᵛ tribes of 'barbarians'ᵛ like the Visigoths and Vandals began to attack its frontiers. Slowly, the Roman Empire became weaker, and by AD 500 it had collapsed.

3 The Holy Roman Empire

One of the barbarian tribes – the Franks – settled in Central France. They were Christians, and after Charlemagne became their leader (see page 22) they quickly conquered a large part of Western Europe. By the time of Charlemagne's death in 814, the 'Holyᵛ Roman Empire' spread from the Pyrenees to modern-day Germany.

4 The Vikings

Again, though, peace and stability didn't last. By 900, several foreign armies were attacking the Holy Roman Empire. One of them belonged to the Vikings, who came from Sweden, Denmark and Norway. The Vikings travelled by sea in 'longboats' and were very successful soldiers. They settled in Ireland, Britain, parts of Russia and also Northern France, where they became known as 'Normans' (north men). In 1066 it was a Norman called 'William the Conqueror' who invaded Britain and became King William I.ᴮᴺ²

A Viking attack

5 The Crusades

Before and during the eleventh century, many Christian Europeans used to visit the Holy Land (modern-day Israel). Then in 1071 Turkish Muslims conquered the area. As a result, Pope Urban II ordered a holy war or 'crusade' in 1095. Four years later, a Christian army captured Jerusalem. There were nine more Crusades in the twelfth century, but none was as successful as the first. Finally, Muslim soldiers regainedᵛ control of Jerusalem in 1187. A century later, the last Christians were forced to leave the Holy Land.

6 The Black Death

Plaguesᵛ were common in the Middle Ages. The worst was 'The Black Death', which reached Sicily from Asia in the 1340s. It was originally brought by rats who lived on ships, and it spread quickly across Europe. A third of the Continent's population died in less than six years.

During the fourteenth century, a third of Europe's population died from The Black Death

European civilisation began over 4,000 years ago. Since then, a long list of...
• empires • wars • triumphs • disasters • ideas • movements, have all
played a part in its development. Here, and over the page, we focus on
twenty of them – each a vital turning point[v] in European history up to 1945.

7 The Hanseatic League

This was an early version of the Common Market. It began in 1241 when two German cities – Hamburg and Lübeck, agreed to protect each other's merchants and trade routes. This agreement or 'Hanse' grew, and by 1400, over 150 cities belonged to it. Together they were known as 'The Hanseatic League' and they traded across Northern Europe. In England they were called 'easterlings' (people who come from the east). A short form of that name – 'sterling' – referred to the Hanse merchants' money. It's still in use today as the name of Britain's currency.

8 Printing

Before the 1450s books were extremely rare. Why? Because each one had to be written by hand. That all changed in 1454, though, when a German – Johannes Gutenberg – introduced Europe's first printing machine or 'press' in the city of Mainz. The result was an information revolution. In the next 50 years, printing presses appeared not only in other parts of Germany, but also in France, Italy, Spain and England. Suddenly, more people than ever before were able to discover the world of learning and ideas.

9 The Renaissance

This was a period of enormous progress in the arts and sciences. It began in Northern Italy during the fifteenth century and was inspired by classical Greek and Roman ideas.

'Renaissance' means 'rebirth' and that's exactly what happened... European culture was reborn. Four of the greatest painters of this time were Leonardo da Vinci (see page 22), Michelangelo, Botticelli[BN3] and Raphael. But the Renaissance wasn't just an age of great art. Astronomy, medicine, architecture, literature and philosophy made major advances, too. And who paid for all this work? Usually, scientists and artists were employed by rich aristocrats or 'patrons'.

10 Exploration

Between 1488-1534, European explorers made some of the greatest voyages in history. They discovered new seas, countries and even continents. For example...

• in **1488** Bartolomeu Dias (Portugal) reached the Cape of Good Hope.
• in **1498** Vasco da Gama (Portugal) became the first European to reach India by sea.
• in **1492** Christopher Columbus (Italy) discovered 'The New World' (in fact what he found was the West Indies).
• in **1499** Amerigo Vespucci (Italy) explored the South American coast. This new continent was named 'America' after him.
• between **1519-21** Ferdinand Magellan (Portugal) sailed around the world, but only 18 of his 250 crew[v] survived.
• between **1519-34** Hernando Cortés (Spain) and Francisco Pizarro (Spain) conquered the Aztecs and Incas in South America.

Columbus landing in the West Indies

History...(2)

11 The Reformation

In the early sixteenth century, the Roman Catholic Church dominated Europe. It was rich, powerful and played a central role in society. But in less than 50 years, half of Western Europe had left the Catholic Church. This dramatic change is called the Reformation. Why did it happen? Well, the main reason was that people began to protest about Church corruption^v. The leader of these protesters or 'Protestants' was a German priest called Martin Luther. He wanted a simple, honest form of Christianity which focused on God – not money or power. Millions agreed with him (including King Henry VIII of England) and by 1560 there were two different kinds of European Christianity – Catholic and Protestant.

12 The Age of Reason

Sir Isaac Newton

Logic and science both made huge progress during the seventeenth and eighteenth centuries. This was 'the age of reason' – a time when new ideas about the world replaced many old beliefs. In England, Sir Isaac Newton discovered the laws of gravity^{v BN4} and motion. In France, Diderot (a philosopher) spent 25 years writing an encyclopaedia^v which contained all human knowledge. And it was another French thinker – Descartes – who defined the age of reason with his phrase, *'I think, therefore I am'.*

13 The Industrial Revolution

During the eighteenth century, Europe's population doubled. Cities grew, fewer people lived in villages, and a new kind of society began to appear. This happened more quickly in Britain than anywhere else. That's because it was the first country to... (a) develop new industrial machines, (b) build factories. The result was that by 1800 Britain dominated world trade and was called 'the workshop^v of the world'. Soon, though, other countries industrialised, too. The age of coal, steam and iron had arrived.

The Bastille was attacked on 14 July, 1789

14 The French Revolution

Between 1789-99 the French people completely changed their political system. The revolution began when Parisian citizens attacked the city's famous Bastille prison. Their demands? A more democratic society based on 'liberty', 'equality' and 'fraternity'. What followed was a decade of rapid and often violent change. Over 40,000 aristocrats, including King Louis XVI and his wife, Marie Antoinette, were killed. The French Revolution both shocked and inspired the rest of Europe. It ended in 1799 when a 30-year-old general – Napoleon Bonaparte (see page 23) – seized^v power.

15 Napoleon

Few individuals have changed European history as much as Napoleon. Like Charlemagne before him and Hitler afterwards, he tried to conquer the entire continent. He nearly succeeded, too – but the armies of several nations finally defeated him in 1815 at the Battle of Waterloo.

16 Science and Transport

In the century after Waterloo, science developed rapidly.
• Louis Pasteur discovered the causes of diseases.
• Charles Darwin (see page 24) wrote his famous book about evolution.
• Sigmund Freud (see page 24) explored the human mind.
• Marie Curie (see page 25) discovered radium.

And that's not all. There was a complete revolution in the world of transport, too. Before 1815, most people travelled on foot, by horse or in a carriage. By <u>19</u>15 they were able to use… • bicycles • cars • trains • steamships • aeroplanes. Things were changing, and changing fast.

17 Empire

Rich European countries had controlled foreign colonies for centuries. During the 1800s and early 1900s, though, their empires grew enormously. Take Africa, for example. Between 1880-1914, it was almost completely divided between… France, Belgium, Spain, Portugal, Britain, Italy and Germany.

Queen Victoria

The largest nineteenth-century European empire belonged to Britain. Ruled by Queen Victoria (1819-1901) it covered 25 per cent of the world's land surface and included 25 per cent of the world's population. Countries in the British Empire included… • India • South Africa • Australia • New Zealand • Canada.

18 World War One – 1914-18

Experts still argue about the causes of World War One, but one thing is certain… it was the worst conflict in Europe's long and often bloody history. Over 30 countries and 65 million soldiers were involved. Of those 65 million, 10 million died and another 20 million were injured – many at battles like the Somme, Verdun and Ypres.

After the war there was a conference at Versailles (near Paris). There, the map of Europe was redrawn. Old empires (Germany/Austria-Hungary/Russia) lost territory, and several newly independent countries (Finland/Lithuania/Poland) were born. No-one could predict the future in 1918, but everyone was certain of one thing – there should never <u>ever</u> be another world war.

19 The Great Depression

This economic crisis began in the USA in 1929 and caused enormous poverty on both sides of the Atlantic. Companies collapsed, banks closed, and millions of people lost their jobs. One result of the Great Depression was the rise of 'fascism'. This was a new, right-wing^v and extremely undemocratic form of politics. Fascist leaders (like Adolf Hitler in Germany and Benito Mussolini in Italy) were men of action who promised to make their countries strong and rich again. During the 1930s they became more and more powerful.

20 World War Two – 1939-45

Less than half a century after the Treaty^v of Versailles, Europe found itself at war again. This time, the conflict was between democracy and the growing power of fascism. It began when Hitler invaded Poland and ended six years later with the defeat of Germany. By then, over 50 million people had been killed or injured. And Europe? For the second time in its twentieth century history, Europe lay in ruins.

Twenty million soldiers were injured during the First World War

VOCAB BOX

corruption – crime committed by people in authority
gravity – the force which makes things fall when they are dropped
encyclopaedia – a book of facts and information arranged alphabetically
workshop – a place where things are made, e.g. a factory
seized – took by force
right-wing – conservative (politically)
treaty – a formal written agreement between two or more countries

1945
Yalta and Potsdam

The shape of post-war Europe was decided at these two conferences. As a result… (a) the Soviet Union was able to control several East European nations, (b) Germany was divided into four areas or 'zones' occupied by France, America, Britain and the USSR.

Churchill, Roosevelt and Stalin at Yalta

1946
The Iron Curtain

During a speech in America, British Prime Minister Winston Churchill described the new East/West division in Europe like this…
'From Stettin in the Baltic to Trieste in the Adriatic, an iron curtain has descended across the Continent.'

1952
ECSC

The 'European Coal and Steel Community' was an attempt by six West European countries to strengthen and protect two of the Continent's most important industries (see pages 10/11).

1957
The EEC

The 'European Economic Community' – a trade alliance between France, West Germany, Italy, Belgium, The Netherlands and Luxembourg – was born.

1961
The Berlin Wall

On Sunday, 13 August 1961, East Germany built a huge wall between East and West Berlin. Why?
(a) To defend Communism from attack,
(b) To stop East Berliners from escaping to the West.
The wall became an international symbol of the Cold War.

1973
The EEC Expands

Three new members – Denmark, Ireland and Britain – joined the European Economic Community.

1989
East-European Communism Collapses

In 1985 Mikhail Gorbachev became the leader of the Soviet Union. He quickly started… (a) to make peace with the West, (b) to reform Communism. One result of these policies was the rapid collapse of Soviet control in Eastern Europe (see pages 12/13). It was one of the twentieth century's most dramatic events. It also led directly to German reunification in 1990.

1992
The Single European Act

The introduction of this law was an important step in the European Community's development. It mean that people, goods and services could move between member countries without any barriers at al

1948
The Berlin Airlift

After the USSR established a Communist 'East Germany', it closed all the roads from the capital, Berlin, to the West. Britain, France and America refused to accept this and delivered goods[v] to Berlin by air instead. This 'airlift' involved hundreds of planes and lasted for twelve months. In the end it was a success – parts of Berlin remained 'Western'.

1949
NATO

In April of this year, the 'North Atlantic Treaty Organisation' was formed. It was (and still is) a military alliance[v] between North American and West European countries. In the same year, Russia exploded its first atomic bomb.

1955
The Warsaw Pact

This was the Communist answer to NATO. Led and dominated by the Soviet Union, its other members were East Germany, Czechoslovakia, Romania, Hungary, Poland, Albania and Bulgaria.

1956
The Hungarian Uprising[v]

During 1956, Hungary tried to free itself from Communist control. The response was brutal.[v] Soviet tanks and soldiers crushed[v] the uprising and over 20,000 Hungarians were killed.

1962
The Cuba Crisis

America (led by John Kennedy) and the Soviet Union (led by Nikita Khrushchev) nearly went to war when Soviet missiles were found near America on the island of Cuba. If war had begun… (a) it would have been nuclear, (b) Europe would almost certainly have been attacked. It was the most dangerous moment of the entire Cold War period.

1968
The Czech Uprising

During the early months of 1968, Czech leader Alexander Dubček introduced several liberal reforms. 'The Prague Spring' was short, though. In August, Soviet tanks occupied Czechoslovakia and Alexander Dubček was removed from power.

1993
The Channel Tunnel

Britain and the Continent have been separated by the English Channel for thousands of years. Well, they're not separated any more. Now, they're connected by a 57-kilometre rail tunnel which is the longest in the world.

VOCAB BOX

post – (here) after
USSR – the Union of Soviet Socialist Republics
Prime Minister – the politician in charge of a government
goods – products
alliance – an agreement between friendly nations
uprising – revolt
brutal – cold, hard and aggressive
crushed – totally and rapidly destroyed
the Cold War – the state of East/West military and political tension before 1989

The European Commu...

Do you know…(a) when the EC began? (b) which cou...
(d) how all the different parts (e.g. the Commission, t...
Well, if you don't – relax – because the N...

How it all began

After World War Two, Europe was weak.

- Millions of its citizens had died.
- The age of Empire was dead.
- Two new superpowers, America and the Soviet Union, now dominated international affairs.

Europe had to find a new role[v]. It began to do this in 1952 with the creation of the European Coal and Steel Community (ECSC). This organisation had six members – France, West Germany, Italy, Belgium, the Netherlands and Luxembourg. Its job? To unite Europe's coal and steel industries. Why? (a) To make them more efficient[v].

(b) To increase profits. (c) To promote peace and co-operation.

Five years later, the same countries went even further. At a conference in Rome they decided to form the European Economic Community (or 'EEC'). This agreement created a 'common market' with… (a) central organisations like the European Commission and the European Parliament to run[v] it, (b) common rules on trade and agriculture which each government in the Community agreed to follow.

The European Commission

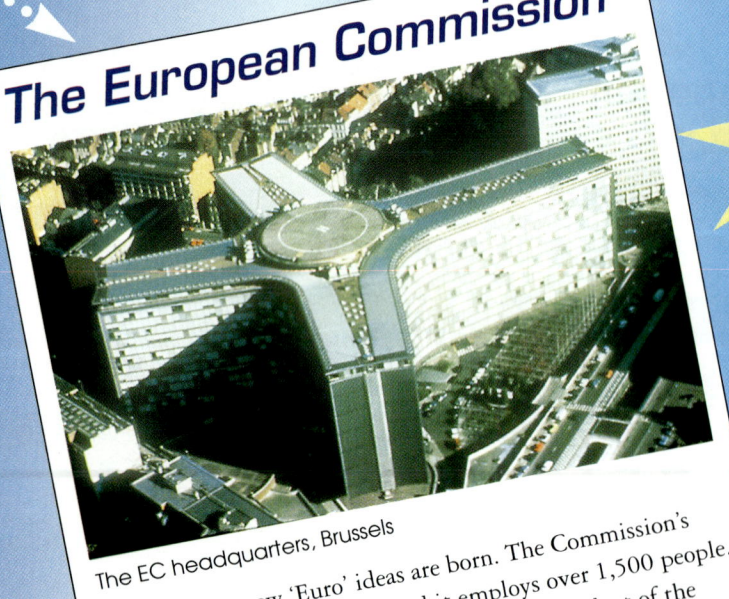

The EC headquarters, Brussels

This is where new 'Euro' ideas are born. The Commission's headquarters are in Brussels and it employs over 1,500 people. The most important of these are… (a) the President of the Commission, (b) seventeen 'Commissioners' – two each from Germany, France, Italy, Britain and Spain – one from each of the other member nations. They serve for four years and are responsible not to their national parliaments, but to the European Parliament.

Ideas come from the Commissioners and their teams or 'cabinets' (each one specialises in a different subject, e.g. trade or agriculture). These ideas are then either accepted or rejected by a majority vote of all the Commissioners. If an idea is accepted, it moves forward to…

The European Parliament

Inside the European Parliament, Strasbourg

Members of the European Parliament (MEPs) are directly elected every five years by voters in their own countries. There are 518 of them:

- France, Britain, Germany and Italy have 81 each.
- Spain has 60.
- The Netherlands has 25.
- Belgium, Greece and Portugal have 24 each.
- Denmark has 16.
- Ireland has 15.
- Luxembourg has 6.

OK – that's where they come from. Now… where do they work and what powers do they have? Well… they work in two different places. (1) **Strasbourg** (in northern France). That's where the main Parliament building is and where debates take place. (2) **Brussels**. The majority of an MEP's job consists of research, meetings and committee work. Most of this happens in the Belgian capital.

As for powers – MEPs can't actually pass laws. What they *can* do, though, is represent the views of ordinary Europeans. The Parliament's… • reports • debates • recommendations… are a vital democratic link between the Commission and…

...es already belong? (c) which ones are waiting to join?
...arliament and the Council of Ministers) actually work?
...'s^v 'beginner's guide' has all the answers.

The Members

France, West Germany, Italy and the Benelux^v countries signed the Treaty of Rome in 1957. Denmark, the UK and Ireland joined the Community sixteen years later in 1973. Greece became a member in 1981, and five years later, so did Spain and Portugal. That made a total of twelve as the 1990s began, but more countries seem certain to join before the year 2000. Austria, Sweden and Turkey have already applied for membership. And then, of course, there are the ex-Communist countries of Central and Eastern Europe. Many experts believe that Hungary, Czechoslovakia and Poland will soon be in the EC, too.

What the EC does

Today's Community (it's usually called the EC now, not the EEC) works hard to promote European business, industry and free trade. It's not *just* an economic organisation, though. These days, EC decisions and laws affect almost every aspect of life in the member countries, including:

• education • employment • energy • the environment • foreign aid^v • human rights • the law • medical and scientific research • transport.

Now let's look at some of the organisations which **propose** (the European Commission), **debate** (the European Parliament) and **take** (the Council of Ministers/Euro-Summits) those decisions.

The Council of Ministers

Government ministers meet regularly

This organisation consists of government ministers from all twelve member countries who meet regularly to talk about Community business. For example, when important agricultural issues (which have come through the Commission and the Parliament) need to be discussed, there's a meeting of the twelve agriculture ministers – when transport issues need to be discussed, the transport ministers meet, and so on.

Most EC decisions are made by the Council of Ministers. Most, but not all. Why's that? Because really central questions are decided at an even higher level – namely at...

Euro-Summits^v

European leaders at a summit meeting

These crucial^v meetings take place three times per year. The people who go to them are
... (a) Heads of State (Presidents and Prime Ministers).
... (b) Foreign Ministers.
It's during summits that the EC's biggest decisions are taken (or sometimes not taken) – for example...
• What will a single European currency mean for the Community?
• Should Europe have a common defence and foreign policy?

The Future

So... that's the end of our brief EC tour. But what about the future? How will the Community develop in years to come? Will there be a European government one day, for example? Maybe even a 'United States of Europe'? Perhaps. Perhaps not. For now, it's too early to say, but one thing is certain – despite all its problems – Europe has never been more united in its long history than it is today.

VOCAB BOX

NED – New Europe Dossier
role – job or position
efficient – able to work hard, well and quickly
run – (here) control/organise
Benelux – short for 'Belgium, the Netherlands and Luxembourg'
foreign aid – money and goods given to foreign countries
summits – (here) meetings between world leaders
crucial – extremely important

THE EAST

Before During After

At the end of World War Two, Russia was determined to protect itself against another invasion. To do this, it built a barrier of six 'satellite'ᵛ countries against the West – East Germany, Poland, Czechoslovakia, Hungary, Romania and Bulgaria – all of which had Communist governments by 1949. The result was a powerful Eastern 'bloc'ᵛ controlled by Moscow for the next 40 years. So what was life like in the satellites during that time? Well, it varied from country to country, of course – each one had its own complex history and its own style of Communism. Basically, though, in all six…

- media propagandaᵛ and a secret police system controlled the population
- the economy was weak
- living standards were low
- foreign travel was almost impossible for ordinary citizens.

Some countries tried to introduce reforms to this harshᵛ system, but without success. Soviet tanks quickly ended rebellions in both Hungary (1956) and Czechoslovakia (1968). Similarly, when Poland's Solidarity trade union became powerful in 1980/82, that too was silenced.

So how was it possible that only eight years later the entire satellite system collapsed? Well – the answer is simple. After Mikhail Gorbachev became Soviet leader in 1985 he decided to stop supporting it. Why? Because…

(a) he wanted to end the Cold War and make peace with the West

(b) the USSR had huge social and economic problems at home. It simply wasn't in a position to dominate foreign satellites any more.

At first, when these new signals came out of the Kremlinᵛ many East Europeans were suspicious. Was it a trick? Could it be true? Slowly, though, they realised that it wasn't a trick. The Soviet Union really was saying, 'Go your own way. We won't stop you.' And that's exactly what they did.

Each of the '89 revolutions was different…
- in East Germany it was largely peaceful
- in Romania it was violent
- in Czechoslovakia it was led by writers and intellectuals
- in Poland most of the leaders came from trade unions and the Catholic Church.

But despite the differences there were similarities, too. One was speed. No-one expected the East European governments to fall so quickly. Another was the important role played by the media. As one East German soldier later described the night the Berlin Wall came down… *'We took our orders from television.'* Thirdly, the revolutions were similar because they all succeeded.

By 1990, powerful Communist leaders like
- Erich Honecker (East Germany)
- Nicolae Ceausescu (Romania)
- Todor Zhivkov (Bulgaria)
- Milos Jakes (Czechoslovakia)

had all been removed from power. Instead, Eastern Europe now had a new generation of politicians – men like Vaclav Havel (Czechoslovakia) and Lech Walesa (Poland). It was a time of enormous optimism and excitement … Communism was dead and anything seemed possible. In reality, though, as the people of Eastern Europe soon realised, revolution didn't mean the end of all their troubles. They might be free, but in many ways, that was just the beginning…

Since '89, the ex-satellite countries have faced a long list of difficult problems. Three of the most serious are unemployment, pollution and nationalism.

- **Unemployment**. East European economies and currencies are very weak compared to those of EC countries. Under the Communist system industries were helped and protected by money from the State.ᵛ Now, though, that protection has gone and in an atmosphere of 'survive or die', many industries are dying. The result is high unemployment in many of the ex-satellites.
- **Pollution**. Before '89, few people realised what a major pollution problem there was in Eastern Europe. Only after the revolutions were scientists able to measure it accurately. Poor quality air, poisoned rivers, dead forests… in some industrial areas, Greenᵛ organisations are calling the situation an 'eco-disaster'.
- **Nationalism**. Many different ethnicᵛ and religious groups lived together under the old Eastern bloc system. Then, they had no choice, but now they want to control their own lives. This has created dangerous political tensions in the East.

Problems like these can't be solved quickly. It takes time to…
- organise democratic political parties
- create new industries and jobs
- improve living standards
- reduce pollution
- settle nationalist disputes.

But despite their difficulties, at least today's Eastern Europeans are free to solve them. And if they *can* solve them, then perhaps something extraordinary will happen. Perhaps in the twenty-first century, Mikhail Gorbachev's dream of a *'common European house'* will come true.

The 1989 revolutions in Eastern Europe were watched by an amazed world. In this four-page report, we first examine... (a) how the former USSR controlled its European allies before '89,
(b) the revolutions themselves,
(c) three major issues now facing the new democracies.

Then, on pages 14/15, you can find out what Eastern Europeans themselves think about life in the 1990s.

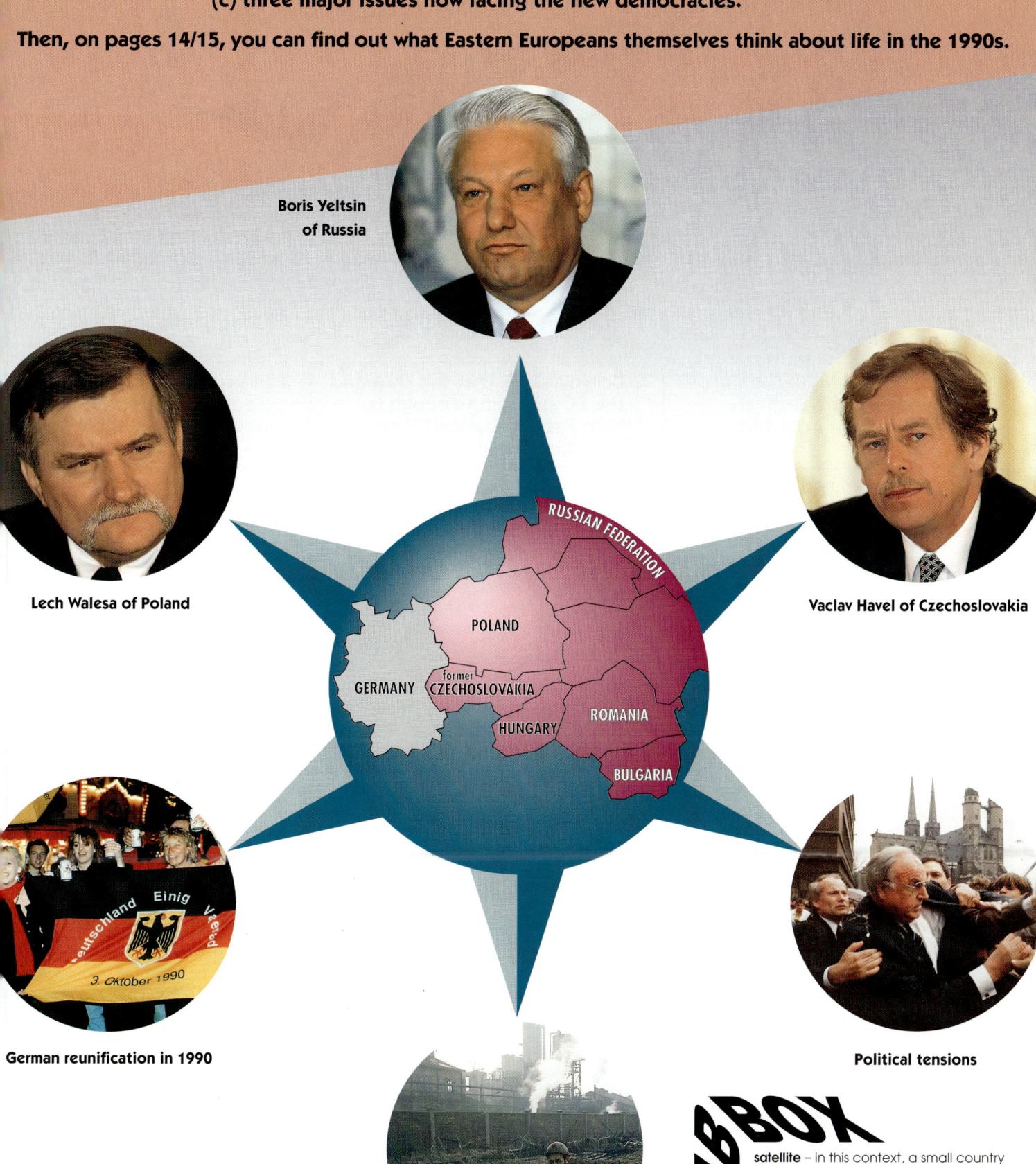

Boris Yeltsin of Russia

Lech Walesa of Poland

Vaclav Havel of Czechoslovakia

RUSSIAN FEDERATION

POLAND

GERMANY former CZECHOSLOVAKIA

HUNGARY

ROMANIA

BULGARIA

German reunification in 1990

Political tensions

Pollution in Poland

VOCAB BOX

satellite – in this context, a small country completely dependent on a larger one
bloc – a group of political parties or nations
propaganda – official (and usually false) information designed to control public opinion
harsh – severe
the Kremlin – a complex of buildings in Moscow, until recently the centre of Soviet government
the State – (here) the government
Green – environmental
ethnic – racial

THE EAST 2

Ques[...]

	1 How has democracy changed everyday life for ordinary people in your country?	2 Do you think that the USA and the EC are doing enough to help Eastern Europe? If not, what else should they do?	3 In your opinion, is the worl[...] a safer place today than it was five years ago?
HUNGARY	'It's difficult for people to change from a passive, supported way of life to an active one. They have to realise that they can do something on their own these days.' 'Life for ordinary people is getting worse at the moment, but I think eventually it will get better.' 'It hasn't changed everyday life. Nothing has really changed except the political system. I never agreed with Communism, but at least people didn't starve[v] in those days.'	'I don't think it's enough, but they can't do more because they have other places to help.' 'What we really need is up-to-date technology and training, not just financial aid thrown into a bottomless pit without control.' 'I think we need more commercial businesses and investments. That's where the West can really help us.'	'No. It's closer to World War Three than it wa[...] 'The world has never been a safe place.' 'Not at all. But I think the world has never b[...] a safe place, and the increasing differen[...] between poor and rich in Europe can o[...] make matters worse.'
POLAND	'People in Poland are not used to democracy in the western sense. They still want the state to make decisions for them and they often act like spoilt[v] children, not mature citizens.' 'Ordinary people are free to express their views. At the same time, however, the market economy[v] which goes with democracy has created "the new poor".' 'There is no censorship[v] on books and newspapers, so information is available everywhere on all kinds of topics. But is that sufficient?'	'I don't believe in other countries' charity. If they're doing anything they're obviously looking for some profit – that's why it's hard to expect them to do more.' 'In my opinion, financial aid should be limited. Instead, Western advisers on economics, finance, law, etc. should help Poland organise her own structures and stand on her own two feet.' 'I think they are doing a lot but not enough.'	'No – especially when you think about the [...] in nationalism in small Eastern Europe[...] countries and the growing lack of tolerance[...] 'Definitely. But of course it depends wh[...] you live… some parts of the world are s[...] than others.' 'Certainly not. With the fall of Commun[...] there's now an American military superpo[...] no longer balanced by the Soviet Union.'
CZECHOSLOVAKIA	'The advantages are that we can say what we want and go where we want. The big disadvantage is that everything is more expensive.' 'What democracy?' 'There are more opportunities and possibilities than before. Also, people aren't afraid of going to prison for their political views.'	'They should help us to improve our educational system.' 'I think the USA and the EC are doing a lot to help us, but they're not helping quickly enough. There's far too much bureaucracy.' 'Yes, but international aid isn't enough. What's really important is for us to help ourselves, not just depend on our rich friends.'	'I think that the world is a safer place beca[...] there are hardly any Communist countries l[...] 'Generally it's safer, but in some areas there [...] still serious problems. Eastern Europe is o[...] the Middle East is another.' 'Obviously there's less risk of a big nuclear [...] between the ex-Soviet Union and Amer[...] Apart from that, though, I think things [...] probably less safe today than five years ag[...]

Hungary – 'It hasn't changed everyday life.'

Eastern Opinions

We asked over 100 students in Czechoslovakia, Poland and Hungary to tell us about their lives. How have things changed since the collapse of Communism? What are their hopes, fears and ambitions? Are they optimistic or pessimistic about the future? Here's a selection of quotes from their replies.

Poland – 'I'm too young to be pessimistic.'

Would you like to change places for six months with a young Western European? If so, why? If not, why not?	5 Do you think it's important to be able to speak English these days? If so, why?	6 Are you optimistic or pessimistic about your country's future in the next ten years? Why?	
...ould go immediately. I have no concept ...orders in my mind. I think I'm European.' ...aybe. I think it's a good way to learn ...guages, but I wouldn't be able to live ...thout my Hungarian friends and my ...ents.' ...s, because I think the only way to get a real ...ture of a country is to live there for a ...le.'	'Yes, I think it's very important because English is the number one language in business and communications.' 'English is popular these days, but in Eastern Europe it's very useful to know German, too.' 'Yes, I need to speak at least one foreign language because very few people abroad can speak Hungarian.'	'When I close my eyes and don't think about the fragile peace surrounding my country, I'm optimistic.' 'I'm optimistic because it couldn't be worse.' 'I'm pessimistic because in reality very little has changed. OK, there's a different government, but politicians are still politicians.'	
... I've lived in the West for a year already ...d the life there is crazy. Everything is ...ntred around[v] money.' ...anging places for six months is one of my ...ams. I wouldn't like to stay there for ever, ...ugh.' ...s – to see what a young Western ...opean's life looks like and to give him/her ... chance to experience life in this part of ...ope.'	'English has become the lingua franca[v] of the world. It's used everywhere in trade, advertising, computers, etc. – so not knowing it is like being sort of illiterate[v].' 'Yes it is. It makes you feel really European.' 'What a self-conceited question!'	'I try not to think about it in terms of optimism or pessimism. I just keep my fingers crossed.' 'Optimistic. I'm too young to be pessimistic.' 'I'm definitely pessimistic. The changes going on all around us are very painful – especially for older people.'	
..., it would be a great chance to have new ...periences and practise my English.' ..., I wouldn't want to live in the West. I think ...miss my own country too much.' ...s. I was in Britain two years ago and I've got ...nds there. I'd love to go back and see them ...in.'	'Yes. We have to make international business contacts and, unless you can speak English, that's really hard to do these days.' 'Yes, because my country is very small and it's in the middle of Europe.' 'It depends. If you just want to live a quiet family life in Czechoslovakia, probably not. But if you're interested in business, travel, international politics or science it's really important.'	'I'm really optimistic because I think, in the '90s, people will have a better chance to develop their skills.' 'Pessimistic. All you have to do is look around you to see the reasons why.' 'Slightly optimistic. Things are changing quickly – perhaps too quickly for some people – but in the end I think we can build a better society.'	

Czechoslovakia – 'I think we can build a better society.'

VOCAB BOX

starve – suffer (or even die) from hunger
spoilt – selfish and childish
the market economy – capitalism
censorship – government control of the arts and media
centred around – focused on
lingua franca – common language (Latin)
illiterate – unable to read or write

Euro-City Highlights

Athens

The Parthenon

No trip to Athens is complete without visiting the Acropolis. The word means 'high city' and it's a hill on which the ancient Greeks built a complex[v] of temples and palaces. One of them – the Parthenon – was a temple dedicated to the goddess Athena[v]. It was completed in 438 BC and although it's in ruins now, it's still one of the world's most beautiful buildings.

Only five minutes walk from the Acropolis is another very old part of Athens – the Plaka. With its narrow streets, restaurants, bars, shops and discos, the Plaka is a popular tourist destination, as is Syntagma Square. This is where you'll find some of the city's most elegant hotels and cafes. It's also near the Parliament and Presidential Palace, which are guarded by soldiers called 'évzones' who wear traditional costumes.

A kilometre south-east of Syntagma Square is the Olympic Stadium. Completed at the end of the nineteenth century, it's made of white marble[v], can seat 70,000 people and was paid for by a millionaire called George Averoff. The first modern Olympic Games[BN5] took place there in 1896.

Finally, anyone interested in Greek culture and history can't afford to miss the National Archaeological Museum. Its unique collection of pots, jewels, sculptures and other classical treasures makes it one of the world's top museums of ancient art.

Berlin

No city symbolises the new Europe more than Berlin. Reunited in 1989, Germany's capital is a fascinating[v] mixture of yesterday, today and tomorrow. What are the main tourist sights? Well – why not start with a walk along the Kurfürstendamm (or 'Ku'damm' for short). Sometimes called 'Berlin's Champs-Élysées', this busy avenue is lined with luxury hotels, shops and night-clubs.

Or, if you prefer something quieter, try a visit to Schloss Charlottenburg. Built between 1695-9 for Sophie Charlotte, Prussia's first queen, it's the city's biggest and loveliest palace. It also has beautiful gardens and is very close to the Egyptian museum where visitors can see Queen Nefertiti's world-famous statue.

A more modern (but still historic) city highlight is the Reichstag. This was Germany's parliament building in the late nineteenth century, but it burned to the ground in 1933. Later it was rebuilt, and today it's used by German politicians again. It also contains a fascinating exhibition called 'Fragen an die Deutsche Geschichte' ('Questions about German History').

History, in fact, is never far away in Berlin. Take the eighteenth-century Brandenburg Gate, for example. Between 1961-89 it was part of the wall which separated West Berlin from the Communist East. And it's there – in the reunited city's eastern half – that you'll find two more highlights… (a) Unter den Linden – a wide boulevard[v] lined with public buildings and linden trees (the name means 'Under the Lindens'), (b) Alexanderplatz (or 'Alex' as everyone calls it) – a busy square which formed the centre of what used to be East Berlin.

Schloss Charlottenburg

Millions of tourists visit European cities every year. After all, from Glasgow to Bucharest it's a continent full of famous buildings, great museums and historic sights. The NED's eight-city tour explores just a few of them.

Budapest

The Parliament Building

Until 1873, Budapest was two separate cities – Buda (on one side of the river Danube) and Pest (on the other). Today, over 20 per cent of all Hungarians live here and it's one of Eastern Europe's most attractive and historic cities. Let's begin our mini-tour at Castle Hill. This is a very old part of the city, with narrow streets, small squares and lots of beautiful, medieval houses. The Royal Palace used to be here, too, but now it's been turned into a collection of museums. Two of them are the National Gallery and the Castle Museum (which tells the story of Budapest itself).

Feeling tired after all that history and culture? OK – why not visit Vörösmarty Tér – a large square in the city centre? It's full of cafes and street musicians – in fact, it's the perfect place to drink coffee and watch the world go by.

Another city highlight – especially in summer – is Margaret Island ('Margitsziget' in Hungarian). Situated in the middle of the Danube, it's a mini-resort^v with its own… • hotels • swimming pool • beach • outdoor theatres.

Finally, two more historic buildings. One is the Parliament, which looks similar to the Houses of Parliament in London and was completed in 1902. The other is the National Museum, which has a wonderful collection of treasures. These include the crown of St Stephen (Hungary's first king) and a conductor's baton^v used by the famous composer, Franz Liszt.

VOCAB BOX

complex (noun) (here) – a group of buildings
Athena – the ancient Greek goddess of wisdom
marble – a kind of stone often used to make statues
fascinating – very interesting
boulevard – a wide avenue
resort – a place where people come to relax and spend their holidays
baton – a short thin stick used to conduct orchestras
displays – (noun) exhibitions
strait – a long, narrow area of water which connects one sea or ocean to another.

Istanbul

Like Berlin, Istanbul is another east/west city. Situated where Europe and Asia meet, it's a busy port full of mosques, markets, palaces and museums. It's not the Turkish capital – that's Ankara – but it *is* the country's largest city (population six million). It's got a long history, too – over 2,500 years. OK – those are a few basic facts. Now… what about the highlights? Well, one of them is definitely 'Aya Sophia' ('Saint Sophia' – the name means 'The Church of Holy Wisdom'). It's one of the world's most beautiful buildings and it was first built by the Roman emperor Constantine. That was in the fourth century and in those days it was a Christian church. A thousand years later, Mehmet II changed it into a Muslim mosque. Then, 500 years after that (in 1935) it became a museum. Now, it's full of both Christian and Muslim treasures.

Another historic and beautiful museum is the Topkapi Palace. This is where Sultans of the Ottoman Empire lived for over 400 years. The name 'Topkapi' means 'Cannon Gate'. That's because two huge guns used to defend the palace. Now, though, visitors are welcome and what they find is a series of fascinating rooms, as well as displays^v of… • weapons • jewels • costumes • pictures • books.

You can't buy any of the Topkapi exhibits, but you *can* spend your money at the Great Bazaar. This is another of Istanbul's main attractions and it's a vast covered market in the city centre. Carpets, clothes, jewels… they're all on offer, along with much, much more.

Finally, one of Istanbul's more modern highlights is the Bosporus Bridge. The Bosporus itself is a narrow strait,^v 30 kilometres long, which separates Europe from Asia. One of the bridges across it – the Bosporus Bridge – is 68m high and 1,074m long – that makes it the longest in Europe.

Aya Sophia

Euro-City Highlights

London

Few cities have more to offer than London. Here are some notes on just seven of its most popular sights.

Buckingham Palace: built in the eighteenth century / a royal home since 1837 / tourists can visit... (a) the Queen's Gallery (a collection of paintings), (b) the Royal Mews (where cars and carriages are kept) / The Changing of the Guard takes place outside every day at 11.30 a.m. (every other day in winter).

10 Downing Street: built in the seventeenth century by Sir George Downing / home of the British Prime Minister / Britain's top economic minister, The Chancellor of the Exchequer, lives next door at number eleven.

Westminster Abbey: Britain's most famous church / kings and queens have been crowned here since the eleventh century / famous writers honoured in 'Poets' Corner'[BN6] include... • Shakespeare • Chaucer • Milton • Hardy • Tennyson • Wordsworth • Keats.

Trafalgar Square: a large square in the city centre or 'West End' / the name comes from a famous 1805 sea battle[BN7] / a statue of the victorious admiral – Lord Nelson – stands on a 52-metre column in the centre of the square.

The South Bank Arts Centre: Europe's largest arts complex / built on the south side or 'bank' of the River Thames / includes... • the Royal National Theatre (drama) • the Hayward Gallery (painting) • the National Film Theatre (cinema) • the Royal Festival Hall (classical music) • the Museum of the Moving Image (a cinema and TV museum).

Covent Garden: a smart and very popular area of shops, cafes and restaurants / home of the Royal Opera House / used to be famous for its fruit and vegetable market.

The Tower of London: built by William the Conqueror (1027–87) as a castle / home of 'The Crown Jewels'[BN8] / the guards wear traditional costumes and are called 'Beefeaters' / the Tower was used as a prison until 1945. Famous prisoners included... • Anne Boleyn and Catherine Howard (two of King Henry VIII's wives) • Sir Walter Raleigh.

Covent Garden

Paris

The glass pyramid outside the Louvre

'The City of Light's' most famous symbol is still the Eiffel Tower. Designed by Gustav Eiffel for the 1889 World Fair, it's visited by millions of people every year and has its own... • restaurant • night-club • bank • post office. 'La Tour Eiffel' isn't the number one tourist attraction in Paris, though. That honour goes to the Pompidou Centre, a high-tech[v] museum of twentieth–century art. Known as 'Beaubourg' by most Parisians, it's one of the city's top three museums. The other two are the Musée d'Orsay (nineteenth-century art) and the Louvre (pre-nineteenth century art). The Musée d'Orsay used to be a railway station. And the Louvre? Well, the Louvre was a royal palace for over 300 years. Now it's the home of masterpieces like the *Venus de Milo*, the *Mona Lisa* and the *Winged Victory*. It also has a new entrance – American architect I.M. Pei's famous 1989 'glass pyramid'. The pyramid is, in fact, one of several major new buildings in Paris. Others include an opera house at La Bastille and a futuristic arch at La Défense.

But let's end our short tour of Paris with two more traditional highlights. One is Notre Dame Cathedral – the beautiful twelfth-century cathedral built on an island in the Seine. The other is Père Lachaise cemetery[v], a fascinating place where the famous inhabitants include... • Chopin (composer) • Balzac (novelist) • Sarah Bernhardt (actress) • Oscar Wilde (playwright) • Jim Morrison (pop singer).

Rome

The Sistine Chapel in the Vatican

Two thousand years ago it was the centre of a huge empire. Now it's only the capital of a single country, but Rome is still one of Europe's most beautiful and historic cities. Here's a short introduction to just four of its many unique sights.

The Forum: This complex of ruined buildings was the centre of power in classical Rome. Politics, the law, religion, the economy… they all had their headquarters in its halls and palaces.

The Colosseum: The Emperor Vespasian (AD 9–79) built this enormous arena[v] in the first century. Inside it, audiences of 55,000 watched a range of violent sports. For example, soldiers called 'gladiators' fought each other with swords and nets, or else lions attacked Christian prisoners. Sometimes there were even sea-battles (when this happened, the floor of the Colosseum was flooded). And here's another interesting fact… During *very* violent contests, audiences used perfume to cover the smell of blood.

The Spanish Steps: These beautiful eighteenth-century steps connect the church of San Trinita dei Monti (at the top) with the Piazza di Spagna (at the bottom). They're very wide and in spring they're almost completely covered in flowers. Why the 'Spanish' steps? Well, that's because of the Spanish Embassy, which has been here since 1647.

One of Rome's most popular and expensive shopping streets – the Via dei Condotti – starts in the Piazza di Spagna.

The Vatican/Saint Peter's Basilica: The Vatican is in Rome, but it's also an independent state (the world's smallest). It's the heart of Roman Catholicism and consists of… • churches • galleries • palaces • offices • libraries • museums.

Its main attraction for many visitors is the ceiling of the Sistine Chapel. This was painted by Michelangelo in the early sixteenth century (it took him twenty months) and is one of western art's great masterpieces.

Nearby is another… St Peter's Basilica. It's from a balcony on this massive[v] church that the Pope addresses pilgrims in St Peter's Square.

Vienna

Austria's capital is the city of Johann Strauss, Sigmund Freud and Gustav Klimt. Highlights include…

Schönbrunn Palace: The Habsburg family ruled Austria for over 600 years. This palace was built for one of them – the Empress Maria Theresa – between 1696–1713. It has over 1,500 rooms and behind it there is a beautiful park. Maria Theresa's daughter – Marie Antoinette – grew up at Schönbrunn before she married King Louis XVI of France in 1770. (She was executed 23 years later during the French Revolution.)

The Prater: The most famous sight in this amusement park is the old ferris wheel or 'Reisenrad', which was built in 1897. It's a symbol of Vienna and appeared in Orson Welles' 1949 film *The Third Man*.

The Staatsoper: Vienna has always been a musical city, and still is today. (Think of the Vienna Philharmonic Orchestra or the Vienna Boys Choir, for example.) The Staatsoper opened in 1869. Now, over 100 years later, it's still one of Europe's most elegant and important opera houses.

Ringstrasse: Before 1858 there was a wall around Vienna. In that year, the Emperor Franz Josef replaced it with a wide, circular boulevard. The modern-day Ringstrasse is lined with monuments, parks, public buildings and museums.

Kärntnerstrasse: You'll find some of Vienna's most expensive shops and cafes on and around this exclusive (and traffic-free)[v] street in the city centre.

The Spanish Riding School: Lipizzaner horses are grey or white. At this internationally-famous Viennese riding school, they (and their riders) are trained to a very high level. But they don't *just* work every day. They also give special performances for visitors.

A Lipizzaner horse from the Spanish Riding School

The Indo-European Story

In the 1780s, a British judge called Sir William Jones was living and working in India. During his time there he studied an ancient language called Sanskrit. What's interesting about that? Well – Sir William noticed something unusual about several Sanskrit words… namely,^v how similar they were to their equivalents in Latin. Take *mother* and *father* for example. In Sanskrit they're *matar* and *pitar*. In Latin they're *mater* and *pater*. Could there, he wondered, be some connection between Sanskrit and Latin?

Over 200 years later experts now believe the answer is definitely 'yes'. Their research shows that between 6000-4500 BC a tribe called the Indo-Europeans settled^v in the northern part of Central Europe. These people kept animals, grew crops and worked with leather and wool. They also had their own language. Until roughly^v 3000 BC this language only existed in Central Europe, but then two things happened. (a) The Indo-Europeans began to ride horses. (b) They discovered the wheel. As a result, they (and their language) began to travel long distances for the first time. Some went east (to India) and some went west (to Scandinavia, Britain and the Mediterranean).

During the next 3000/4000 years, languages like Sanskrit and Latin developed in these new areas – each with its own local vocabulary,

Sir William Jones

Did all Europeans once speak the same language?

expressions and grammar. Meanwhile, as they became stronger, Indo-European itself became weaker, until in the end it disappeared completely. It's a curious thought, isn't it, that modern-day Italian, Danish and Greek all had a common ancestor^v and that in the past all Europeans spoke the same language? Curious – but true.

Longest Words

The list below contains some of Europe's longest words. Why not take a deep breath and see if you can pronounce them?

Language	Word	Meaning
Spanish	Superextraordinarisimo	extraordinary
French	Anticonstitutionellement	anti-constitutionally^v
Italian	Precipitevolissimevolmente	as fast as possible
Turkish	Cekoslovakyalılastıramadıklarımızdanmısınız	are you one of those people who we couldn't Czechoslovakianize?
Dutch	Kindercarnavalsoptochtvoorbereldingswerkzaamheden	preparations for a children's carnival procession
German	Donaudampfschiffartselectrizitaetenhauptbetriebswerkbauunterbeamtengesellschaft	the name of a pre-1939 club in Vienna

...GUAGE

From Norwegian to Spanish and from Dutch to Serbo-Croat, there are over 30 different European languages. But where did they all come from originally? The NED investigates. Plus, we look at… (a) some of the continent's *longest* words, (b) Europe's favourite <u>second</u> language.

Euro-English

The most popular second language in Europe today is English. Perhaps you already knew that (after all, you speak it yourself). But did you also know that English has borrowed thousands of words from other European languages? Here are some examples.

Language	Words
Czech	robot / pistol
Dutch	yacht / wagon / boss / landscape
French	prison / parliament / soup / cigarette / garage
German	kindergarten / hamburger / waltz / delicatessen / seminar^v
Hungarian	coach / paprika^v
Italian	violin / umbrella / cartoon / carnival / solo
Spanish	mosquito / cargo / patio / guerilla / potato

Does anyone here speak English?

Alright… you're on holiday in a European country where you can't speak the language. You *can* speak English though. How do you find out if there are any other English speakers about? You ask, of course. The ten sentences below all mean *'Does anyone here speak English?'* in different languages. The question is… which languages? Choose from the list on the right, then check your answers at the bottom of the page.

1	Spricht hier jemand Englisch?		(a)	Finnish
2	Puhuuko kukaan englantia?		(b)	Portuguese
3	C'è qualcuno qui che parla l'inglese?		(c)	Norwegian
4	Spreekt er hier iemand Engels?		(d)	Spanish
5	Y-a-t-il quelqu'un ici qui parle Anglais?		(e)	Danish
6	Alguém fala inglês?		(f)	Greek
7	Er det noen her som snakker engelsk?		(g)	Dutch
8	¿ Hay alguien aquí que hable inglés?		(h)	German
9	Mila kanis anglika?		(i)	Italian
10	Er der nogon her, der taler engelsk?		(j)	French

"Does anyone here speak English?"

VOCAB BOX

namely – that's to say
settled – (here) made their home
roughly – approximately
ancestor – a relative who lived hundreds of years ago
anti-constitutionally – against a country's basic laws
seminar – a formal academic discussion between a small number of people
paprika – a spice

21

Europe has produced many legendary[v] names. Scientists, artists, politicians, writers… people whose lives and work changed the history of the world.

Plato
Born c[v]428 BC – died c347 BC
Nationality: Greek

This famous philosopher was a student of Socrates. He came from a rich Athenian family, but didn't spend his entire life in Greece. After Socrates' death in 399 BC he travelled widely in Egypt and Italy for over ten years. Then, in 387 BC he returned to Athens and opened the 'Academy'. This was a kind of university for politicians, scientists and philosophers. Plato worked and taught at the Academy until his own death 40 years later.

He wrote over 30 books, including *The Republic, The Symposium* and *The Phaedo*. In them he explored ideas about politics, love, art and morality. Most of his books are 'dialogues' in which the characters talk to each other. These were often performed like plays by Plato's students, who included Aristotle.

Charlemagne
Born 742 – died 814
Nationality: Frankish (French)

Charlemagne, which is short for 'Charles Le Magne' (Charles The Great) became king of a tribe called the Franks in 768. For the next 30 years he struggled to make Western Europe a Christian Empire. To do this he fought battles in Italy, Germany, The Netherlands and Northern Spain. Finally, on Christmas Day 800, Pope Leo III crowned him 'Holy Roman Emperor'.

For the next fourteen years, Charlemagne controlled his huge empire from the city of Aachen (near modern-day Cologne). He introduced new laws, improved the education system and promoted religion. Also, although he himself couldn't read, he took a great interest in books. The Holy Roman Empire lasted 1,000 years after his death until Napoleon ended it in 1806.

Leonardo da Vinci
Born 1452 – died 1519
Nationality: Italian

Today, when we think of the Renaissance (or 'rebirth') we usually think of great paintings. But it wasn't just an age of artistic discovery. It was a period of major scientific change, too. That's why Leonardo da Vinci is so important, because he was both an artist and a scientist. As well as painting masterpieces[v] like *The Mona Lisa, The Last Supper* and *The Virgin Of The Rocks*, he also… • designed helicopters and cathedrals • drew mountains and war-machines • studied how birds fly, rivers flow and the human body works. Most of his ideas are contained in a series of notebooks (which he wrote from right to left). He died in France at the age of 67.

opeans (1)

Our special four-page report on Great Europeans covers more than 2,000 years and takes us from Plato to Picasso.

Napoleon
Born 1769 – died 1821
Nationality: French

Shakespeare
Born 1564 – died 1616
Nationality: British

Mozart
Born 1756 – died 1791
Nationality: Austrian

Britain's most famous playwright[v] was born in the town of Stratford-upon-Avon. At the age of eighteen he married a local girl called Anne Hathaway. Then, two years later, he went to London and began working in the theatre. His career as a dramatist continued for the next 30 years. In that time he wrote almost 40 plays in three main groups – histories, comedies and tragedies.

The histories include…
• *Richard III* • *Henry V* • *Julius Caesar.*
The comedies include…
• *Twelfth Night* • *A Midsummer Night's Dream*
• *All's Well That Ends Well.*
The tragedies include…
• *Hamlet* • *Macbeth* • *King Lear.*

Today, Shakespeare's plays are still popular all over the world. In Britain, the 'Royal Shakespeare Company' (RSC) regularly perform his work in both Stratford and London.

Wolfgang Amadeus Mozart began to write music at the age of five. One year later, his father – Leopold – took him on the first of several European tours. During these visits abroad, Wolfgang played for kings, queens, princes and princesses. He also continued to compose.[v] But he wasn't just a 'child genius'. He worked hard all his life, producing a vast amount of music before he died at the age of 35. The list includes…• 27 piano concertos • 23 string quartets • 20 operas (e.g. *Don Giovanni, Cosi Fan Tutte, The Marriage of Figaro* and *The Magic Flute*) • over 50 symphonies.

Today, everything Mozart wrote has a 'K' number. The K is short for Köchel – a nineteenth-century Austrian who listed all Mozart's work according to when it was written.

Napoleon Bonaparte was born on the island of Corsica. He first became famous as a general during and after the French Revolution. In 1799 he took control of the government in Paris. Five years later he became Emperor. In the decade[v] that followed he introduced a series of reforms (many of them are still a part of French law). He also fought a series of wars against Austria, Russia, Spain, Prussia, and (his most frequent enemy) England.

In 1814 France was invaded and Napoleon was sent to the island of Elba (near Italy) as a prisoner.[BN9] He escaped, though, and took control of the French army again. This period – 'The Hundred Days' – ended with his defeat at the Battle of Waterloo in 1815. After that, Napoleon was sent to another island – St Helena (in the Atlantic). This time he didn't escape and died there in 1821. His body was brought back to France in 1840. Today, it lies in the Hôtel des Invalides (a museum) in Paris.

VOCAB BOX

legendary – extremely famous
c – circa (Latin for 'around' or 'approximately')
masterpieces – important works of art
playwright – someone who writes plays
compose – write (music)
decade – a period of ten years

Darwin
Born 1809 – died 1882
Nationality: British

Marx
Born 1818 – died 1883
Nationality: German

Freud
Born 1856 – died 1939
Nationality: Austrian

This famous Briton studied biology at Cambridge University. Then, between 1831-6 he travelled to South America on a scientific ship called the *Beagle*. In those five years, Charles Darwin observed how animals develop or 'evolve' from generation to generation. He noticed that the strong members of each type or 'species' survived and the weak ones didn't. He also noticed that different species were often very similar, like the members of a family.

Over 20 years later, Darwin published a book. It was called *On the Origin of Species By Means of Natural Selection* and it caused a sensation. Why? Because in it Darwin stated˅ that human beings hadn't always been human beings. Thousands of years ago they were monkeys and had evolved into people. This made many religious groups very angry and started a huge debate. Who was right – Darwin or the Bible? In some parts of the world it's an argument which still continues today.

The father of Communism was born in a town called Trier. He studied law, history and philosophy at Bonn and Berlin. Then, after a period as editor of a newspaper (the *Rheinische Zeitung*), he moved to Paris in 1843. There, he met Friedrich Engels – a political philosopher – and the two men became good friends. Together, they began to develop a new system of political ideas. They wanted to create a different, fairer society – one controlled by ordinary workers, not just a few rich industrialists and aristocrats. They wanted, in other words, a Communist state. Marx and Engels explained their ideas in a book – *The Communist Manifesto* (1848).

Marx moved to London with his wife Jenny the following year. There he continued to promote 'the class struggle'. In 1867 he published the first volume of his most famous book – *Das Kapital*. It was about money, power, the class system and revolution.

Marx died in 1883 and is buried in north London's Highgate Cemetery. He never saw the Communist revolution he dreamed of, but it did happen... in Russia, 34 years after his death.

How does the human mind work? What do dreams mean? Is there a link between childhood events and adult problems? Sigmund Freud spent over 50 years trying to answer questions like these. He was the first psycho-analyst and one of history's most famous doctors. Famous, but not always popular. In fact during his own life, many people attacked his ideas and methods.

Freud worked in Vienna from 1886-1938. During those 52 years he... (a) 'analysed' thousands of patients, (b) wrote several important books, including *The Interpretation of Dreams*, (c) inspired a new generation of psycho-analysts, including Alfred Adler and Carl Jung. In 1938 he left Vienna and moved to London, where he died of cancer˅ the following year. Today, there are Freud museums in both cities.

Picasso
Born 1881 – died 1973
Nationality: Spanish

Emmeline Pankhurst
Born 1858 – died 1928
Nationality: British

Marie Curie
Born 1867 – died 1934
Nationality: Polish

'Votes For Women!' That was the slogan[v] of 'The Women's Social and Political Union' – an organisation started by Mrs Emmeline Pankhurst in 1903. When the twentieth century began, British women didn't have the right to vote. Mrs Pankhurst – a widow[v] with two daughters – decided to change all that. She started the WSPU and became its leader. What did the WSPU do? Well, its members (they were called 'suffragettes')... • held meetings and debates • demonstrated in the streets • wrote articles. Some suffragettes went even further and attacked public property. Many tied themselves to famous buildings with chains. One woman – Emily Davidson – even threw herself under King George V's horse in the 1913 Derby[v] and died.

Over 1,000 suffragettes, including Emmeline Pankhurst, went to prison for their beliefs. There, many of them refused to eat and were 'force-fed'[v] by the guards. Finally, on 10th January 1918, the British government changed its mind and gave women over the age of 30 the right to vote. In 1928 the age was lowered to 21. Mrs Pankhurst died a short time after this final victory.

Maria Sklodowska was born in Warsaw, but at the age of 24 she left Poland and became a student of maths and physics in Paris. There she met and married another scientist – Pierre Curie. Maria (or 'Marie' as everyone now called her) had two children but continued her career after they were born. Then in 1902 her life changed completely when she and Pierre made a fantastic scientific breakthrough.[v] They discovered a new element[v] called 'radium', which was important because doctors could use it to help people with cancer. The Curies didn't use their success (they were awarded the 1903 Nobel Prize [BN10] for Physics) to become rich, though. They continued to work hard and make new discoveries. Marie even continued her research after Pierre died tragically young in 1906. She became a professor of physics at the Sorbonne and in 1911 won a second Nobel Prize – this time for Chemistry. When she herself died in 1934, she was one of the world's best-known scientists.

The twentieth century's greatest artist grew up in Spain but spent three-quarters of his life in France. That's where, between 1901-7, he painted the pictures in his famous 'Blue' and 'Rose' periods. Then, during the next seven years, he and his friend Georges Braque developed a completely new style. It was called 'Cubism' and one critic described it as *'a totally new way of seeing'*. Influenced by African art, Cubism started a revolution in European painting. It also made Pablo Picasso an international star, which is exactly what he remained for the next 60 years. During that time he produced thousands of drawings, sculptures, designs, collages[v] and, of course, paintings. Two of his best-known pictures are *Les Demoiselles d'Avignon* (1907) and *Guernica* (1937).

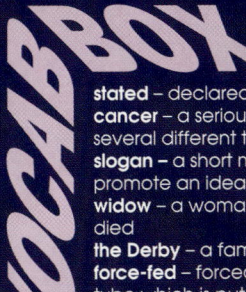

VOCAB BOX

stated – declared (an opinion or a fact)
cancer – a serious illness. There are several different types.
slogan – a short message used to promote an idea or product
widow – a woman whose husband has died
the Derby – a famous British horse-race
force-fed – forced to eat through a tube which is put either up the nose or down the throat
breakthrough – a sudden and important discovery
element – (here) a basic chemical substance (e.g. oxygen or sulphur) which can't be made any simpler
collages – pictures made from pieces of paper, photos, small objects, etc.

There are more European competitions, awards, festivals, courses, exchanges and events today than ever before. Together, they represent a new kind of Euro-culture. There's the 'European Young Musician of the Year' contest, for example. Or the 'European Film Awards'. Then what about the various European sports championships? Or – on another level – the growing number of student exchanges between schools and colleges in different countries?

MUSIC

The Eurovision Song Contest

Some people love it – others hate it – but, worldwide,[v] over a billion[v] TV viewers watch the Eurovision Song Contest every year. The first one took place in 1956. Since then the three countries who've won most often have been France, Luxembourg (five times each) and Britain (four times). Not that Eurovision guarantees chart success or a long career… plenty of winners have been completely forgotten in a matter of months. Others have been luckier, though… think of Bucks Fizz, for example (they won with *Making Your Mind Up* in 1981) or perhaps the most successful Eurovision group of all time – Abba (they won with *Waterloo* in 1974).

Critics of the contest say that it's musically boring – all the songs are either old-fashioned, ridiculous or both. Fans, of course, completely disagree. But whether you think it's worth *'douze points'* or *'deux points'*, one thing is clear… the Eurovision Song Contest is Europe's number one musical event.

Sweden's 'Abba' who won the 1974 Eurovision Song Contest

SPORT

The European Cup

Like the Eurovision Song Contest, this event also took place for the first time in 1956. It's Europe's most important football championship and only the top teams in each country can compete for it. The next page begins with a list of winners.

The European Cup

This report examines three very different aspects of this new Euro-culture. One is a football championship… another is a university degree course… but first, let's start with Europe's (in fact the world's) most popular annual song contest.

The European Cup Final 1991

1956 – Real Madrid (Spain)	**1968** – Manchester United (England)	**1980** – Nottingham Forest (England)
1957 – Real Madrid (Spain)	**1969** – A.C. Milan (Italy)	**1981** – Liverpool (England)
1958 – Real Madrid (Spain)	**1970** – Feyenoord Rotterdam (Holland)	**1982** – Aston Villa (England)
1959 – Real Madrid (Spain)	**1971** – Ajax Amsterdam (Holland)	**1983** – Hamburger S.V. (Germany)
1960 – Real Madrid (Spain)	**1972** – Ajax Amsterdam (Holland)	**1984** – Liverpool (England)
1961 – Benfica (Portugal)	**1973** – Ajax Amsterdam (Holland)	**1985** – Juventus (Italy)
1962 – Benfica (Portugal)	**1974** – Bayern Munich (Germany)	**1986** – Steaua Bucharest (Romania)
1963 – A.C. Milan (Italy)	**1975** – Bayern Munich (Germany)	**1987** – F.C. Porto (Portugal)
1964 – Inter Milan (Italy)	**1976** – Bayern Munich (Germany)	**1988** – P.S.V. Eindhoven (Holland)
1965 – Inter Milan (Italy)	**1977** – Liverpool (England)	**1989** – A.C. Milan (Italy)
1966 – Real Madrid (Spain)	**1978** – Liverpool (England)	**1990** – A.C. Milan (Italy)
1967 – Glasgow Celtic (Scotland)	**1979** – Nottingham Forest (England)	**1991** – Red Star Belgrade (Yugoslavia)

Education
Modern European Studies

University College London (UCL) is the oldest and largest of several colleges in the University of London. It has about 8,500 students and offers a wide variety of degree subjects, including 'Modern European Studies'. What exactly does MES involve? The NED decided to find out.

Q: *How long does the course last?*

A: Four years

Q: *What does it consist of?*

A: Well, that depends. Lots of different languages and special topics are on offer. Every student chooses the combination^v which suits him or her best.

Q: *Everyone has to study a foreign language, though – is that right?*

A: Yes, that's right. In fact some people study two. They can choose from a long list which includes Dutch, French, German, Italian, Spanish and Swedish.

Q: *And what about these 'topics' you mentioned? What are they?*

A: They're subjects which are related to the languages – for example… • literature • geography • economics • business studies • history • law.

Q: *I see. So the course is a mixture of language work and background studies. What about foreign travel – is that involved, too?*

A: Yes. It's a very important part of the course. Students spend their third year abroad,
  – studying at a university.
  – teaching as a language assistant in a school.
  – working in a factory or office.

Q: *And at the end of the fourth year, what qualification do successful students get?*

A: A Bachelor of Arts (BA) degree.

VOCAB BOX

worldwide – around the world
billion – a thousand million
combination – mixture

'VOX'

What do Europeans themselves think of the New Europe?
Here are six contrasting^v *opinions – each from a different country. Some are positive – some not so positive. Which ones do you agree or disagree with? Why? Finally (and most important of all)*
… what do <u>you</u> think?

1 Dieter (Germany)

I'm very optimistic about the New Europe. Now that the Cold War is over, I think the opportunities for peace and prosperity^v are enormous. Not straight away,^v perhaps – it will take several years to solve some of the economic problems in the East, for example – but eventually. And as quickly as possible, really, because Europe *must* be united to compete with Japan and America in the future. 'Together we stand, divided we fall' – that's what the proverb says, isn't it? Well, in Europe's case, I think it's absolutely true.

2 Elsa (Sweden)

As far as I'm concerned, all the talk about Europe these days is incredibly boring. I mean, be honest – who actually cares about it apart from politicians and people in the media? None of my friends do, I can tell you that; and I agree with them. After all, why *should* we be interested in a lot of middle-aged politicians in Brussels? Our lives are here, not there. Not that I'm *against* the EC or anything – I'm not saying that. I'm just fed up with constantly hearing about it, that's all.

3 Laszlo (Hungary)

I think your views on Europe depend on where you live and how much you earn. Rich people in the West can afford to feel confident and idealistic. Here in the East, though, things are different. For us, you see, the problem is that we feel like second-class citizens. We're Europeans, but poor Europeans, and it's going to stay that way for quite a while. OK — there's more freedom now, and that's wonderful – but to be honest, freedom's just the beginning. Food in the shops, secure^v jobs and clean air to breathe – those are the immediate priorities here. Maybe when we've got those, then we'll feel more hopeful about the future.

4 Craig (Britain)

I support co-operation between European countries 100 per cent, what I *don't* support is the idea of a 'United States of Europe'… some kind of super-state with a central government. Why? Because in my opinion each country should keep its basic independence. That's how it's always been in the past and I just don't see the advantage of changing now. If Europe had one language and culture like America, maybe it could work. That's not the reality, though. We're friends and allies, but there's no point pretending we're all the same. We're not.

5 Rosie (Ireland)

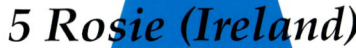

What do I think about the New Europe? Well, personally, I'm all in favour of it – especially the changes in the old Eastern bloc countries. I've got a pen-pal in Warsaw, you see, and next spring she's coming to stay with me and my family for two weeks. Something like that would have been almost impossible to organise a few years ago, but it isn't now. Who knows? – maybe I'll even visit her home in Poland one day. Because that's what really matters, isn't it? – contact between people.

6 Valentina (Italy)

If you look at Europe historically, what's going on today is unique. To me that's the most amazing thing. I mean, just think of the two World Wars. They both started because of divisions inside Europe and what happened?… millions of people died. If we've got the chance to stop that ever happening again, why not take it? Why not work together instead of against one another? OK – there are still going to be problems – of course there are. But then there will *always* be problems. What matters is that inside a united Europe they'll be solved by committees and summits, not guns and bombs.

VOCAB BOX

contrasting – varied
prosperity – wealth
straight away – immediately
secure – safe and reliable

THE PROJECT FILE

OK – you've read the New Europe Dossier. Now it's over to you. Here are six ideas for New Europe projects. They're a lot of fun and they'll help you to practise your English, too. You can do them… (a) on your own (b) with a friend (c) in a group.

EURO-QUESTIONNAIRE

What do the people in your school/college/family/local area think of today's European issues? Are they in favour of a single European currency, for example? What about a central EC government with one defence policy[v] for all the member nations? Then there are the countries of central and eastern Europe. Should they be allowed to join the EC… (a) straight away, (b) only when their economies are much stronger? To find out, write a questionnaire.

(a) Ask approximately ten questions as clearly and simply as possible.

(b) At the end of each question, include a range of possible answers. For example… **YES ☐ NO ☐ DON'T KNOW ☐**, or **SOON ☐ IN FIVE TO TEN YEARS ☐ AT SOME STAGE IN THE FUTURE ☐ NEVER ☐**.

(c) Distribute at least 20 questionnaires, and when they've been filled in[v], check the answers… (How many people ticked 'A' in question 1? How many ticked 'B'? etc). Combine the answers in a list of statistics for each question – e.g.… **QUESTION 1. 45% of people think X. 30% of people think Y. 25% of people think Z.**

(d) Finally, send the completed results of your questionnaire to either…
  (1) Your MEP (Member of the European Parliament) if you live in Europe.
  (2) Your school or college magazine/local paper/the European Commission (see 'Useful Addresses') if you live outside Europe.

MEGA-MAP

There's a map of Europe on page 2 of this Dossier, but it only contains a limited amount of information. Why not make a larger (at least 1-metre square) more detailed map for your bedroom/classroom wall? Here are some suggestions to help you.

(a) Use an English-language atlas to find information not in this Dossier – e.g. the names of seas, oceans, rivers, lakes, mountains, etc.

(b) Leave a wide border around the edge of the map. Fill this with extra data about each country – e.g. 'Language', 'Currency', 'Flag', etc.

You can also decorate the border with… • stamps • postcards • photos from travel brochures/magazines.

(Alternatively, if you don't want to include the whole of Europe in your Mega-Map, focus in more detail on a single country.)

U • S • E • F • U • L   A •

1 **Commission of the European Communities**
Rue de la Loi 200
1049 Brussels
Belgium

2 **The European Parliament**
General Secretariat
Centre Européen
Plâteau du Kirchberg
PO Box 1601
Luxembourg

3 **Erasmus Bureau**
Rue d'Arlon 15
B-1040 Brussels
Belgium

Section

TODAY'S 'GREAT EUROPEANS'

The twelve famous men and women featured on pages 22→25 are all historical figures. But what about more recent heroes and heroines? Who, in your opinion, are the 'Great Europeans' of today? Write twelve mini-profiles˅ of your dozen celebrities. Include (a) a mixture of men and women, (b) a mixture of nationalities, (c) a mixture of professions (i.e. not twelve pop stars or twelve politicians). When you've finished, compare notes with your friends/the other students in your class. How many names on your list also appear on theirs?

CURRENT-AFFAIRS SCRAPBOOK

Europe is constantly in the news these days. • Summits • crises • proposals • conflicts • treaties • new laws – they're all reported at length by newspapers and magazines (as well as on the TV, of course). One way to follow and understand stories like these in detail is to keep a European 'Current-Affairs Scrapbook'. There are two different ways to do this project. You can either… (a) focus on European issues in general, (b) focus on a specific topic, for example… • the environment • tourism • animals • science • sport. Here's what you do.
(a) Read as many different papers and magazines as possible.
(b) Cut out (or photocopy) any interesting 'Euro'-articles.
(c) Stick them into your scrapbook.
(d) Write short English-language captions˅ beside each article. Include the following information in your captions… • when the article was printed • what it's about • its main points.

DOSSIER QUIZ

The New Europe Dossier is packed with˅ information… there are hundreds of dates, facts and figures in its 32 pages. The question is… how much of that information do Dossier readers actually *remember*? To find out, test your friends/the other students in your class by giving them a 'Dossier Quiz'. It should contain 40 questions – ten in each of four different categories…
(a) True or False?
(b) Fill in the blanks.
(c) Multiple choice.
(d) Who said…?

FUTURE FILE

In 'The Modern Age' (pages 8/9) we looked at the last 50 years of European history. But how about the next 50 years? What do you think is going to happen in the first half of the twenty-first century? Write and illustrate a 'Future File' which describes some of the key events –
e.g.… • treaties • international crises • scientific breakthroughs
• the environment • new organisations • economic developments • travel.

VOCAB BOX

policy – a political party's ideas and plans on a specific subject
filled in – (here) completed
mini-profiles – short biographies
captions – short pieces of text which describe a photo or illustration
packed with – full of

• D • R • E • S • S • E • S

4 **Lingua**
   Place du Luxembourg 2/3
   B-1040 Brussels
   Belgium

5 **European Community Youth**
   Exchange Bureau
   Place du Luxembourg 2/3
   B-1040 Brussels
   Belgium

6 **University College London**
   (Admissions Enquiry Office)
   Gower Street
   London WC1E 6BT

See page 32 for more information on these addresses.

1 Pages 2/3

NETHERLANDS There are actually two capital cities in the Netherlands: Amsterdam is the legal and administrative capital, while The Hague is the seat of government.

2 Pages 4/5

THE BATTLE OF HASTINGS William the Conqueror defeated England's King Harold near Hastings, a small town on the south coast. A famous French tapestry[v] tells the story of William's journey to England and his victory at Hastings. It's called the Bayeux Tapestry.

3

BOTTICELLI This Renaissance painter's real surname was Filipepi. 'Botticelli' means 'little barrel' in Italian and was a nickname.[v]

4 Pages 6/7

SIR ISAAC NEWTON According to legend, Sir Isaac Newton (1642–1727) discovered the laws of gravity in a very unusual way. He was sitting under a tree one day when an apple fell on his head.

5 Pages 16/17

THE OLYMPIC GAMES There's a separate Macmillan Dossier about the Olympic Games.

6 Pages 18/19

POETS' CORNER There are plaques[v] and monuments to many of Britain's most famous poets, playwrights and novelists in this small section of the Abbey. The first was a monument to Geoffrey Chaucer (c 1340–1400). Most of them aren't actually buried in Westminster Abbey, though.

7

THE BATTLE OF TRAFALGAR On 21st October 1805, Britain defeated the Franco-Spanish (French and Spanish) fleet[v] off Cape Trafalgar, a few miles from Gibraltar. It was one of the most important sea battles ever fought. The British fleet was led by Lord Nelson (1758–1805) who was killed during the conflict.

8

THE CROWN JEWELS This world-famous collection of jewels belongs to Britain's Royal Family. It's one of the biggest tourist attractions in London and includes eight different crowns.

9 Pages 22/23

ELBA A 'palindrome' is a word or phrase which is exactly the same backwards as well as forwards. One of the most famous palindromes in English is 'Able was I ere[v] I saw Elba'.

10 Pages 24/25

THE NOBEL PRIZE Alfred Nobel (1833–1896) was a Swedish scientist who invented dynamite. Six different 'Nobel' prizes are awarded every 10th December (the anniversary of Nobel's death). They are for physics, chemistry, medicine, economics, literature and peace.

Address Information

3/4/5: Erasmus/Lingua/The European Community Youth Exchange Bureau
The EC organises a wide range of education and training programmes.

Erasmus helps EC students and teachers in higher education to work in other Community countries.

Lingua promotes the learning of foreign languages throughout the EC.

The European Community Youth Exchange Bureau helps students (aged 15–25) and young people with jobs (aged 18–28) to swap places for a few weeks or months with citizens in another part of the Community.

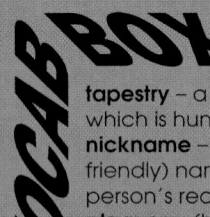

VOCAB BOX

tapestry – a kind of carpet which is hung on the wall
nickname – an informal (usually friendly) name used instead of a person's real name
plaques – (here) flat pieces of stone with information about a person, place or event carved on them
fleet a large group of ships
ere – before (ere is an old-fashioned word no longer used)

The author and publishers wish to acknowledge, with thanks, the following photographic sources:

Allsport pp26 above; 27 above (David Cannon): BBC Enterprises p26 above: The Bridgeman Art Library pp6 left (John Bethell); 6 right (Musée Carnavalet, Paris); 7 above (Christopher Wood Gallery, London); 23 centre (Giraudon); 23 right (Musée des Beaux-Arts, Liège): Camera Press pp15 above (J Kopec); 25 left (Bassano): C.M. Dixon pp4 above left; 22 left: Sally and Richard Greenhill p18 below: Robert Harding Photograph Library p16 below: Hulton-Deutsch Collection pp20 left; 22 right; 24 left; 24 centre; 24 right (Bettmann); 25 centre; 25 right: The Image Bank p11 left (Michael Haynes): Peter Kent p21 above: Magnum pp7 below (Sebastiao Salgado); 13 below (Bruno Barbey); 14 (Stuart Franklin); 16 above (Constantine Manos); 17 above (Abbas): Peter Newark's Historical Pictures pp4 above right and below; 5; 7 below; 22 centre; 23 left: Rex Features pp8 above and below; 9 above and centre; 11 right; 13 above, left, right; 15 below; 17 below; 18 above; 19 above: Alan Thomas pp20 right; 21 below; 28; 29: Topham Picture Source pp contents (Associated Press); 10 left and right; 13 left (Associated Press), 19 below: University College, London p27 below.

The cover photograph is courtesy of The Image Bank, London/Robert Kristofik.

The publishers have made every effort to trace the copyright holders, but if they have inadvertently overlooked any, they will be pleased to make the necessary arrangements at the first opportunity.

Design and artwork by Jordan and Jordan, Fareham, Hampshire

© Macmillan Publishers Limited 1992

Printed in Singapore